THE HIDDEN

A True Story of th

Lola Rein Kaufman
With Lois Metzger

SCHOLASTIC INC.
New York Toronto London Auckland
Sydney Mexico City New Delhi Hong Kong

ISBN 978-0-545-20053-0

12 11 10 9 8 7 6   13 14 15/0

Printed in the U.S.A.   40
This edition first printing, March 2010

THE HIDDEN GIRL
A True Story of the Holocaust

Lola Rein Kaufman
With Lois Metzger

Inside the barn, next to the wooden wall, is a trapdoor that leads down to a root cellar with brick walls. There are bins for potatoes and a dirt floor with straw on it. Anna pushes aside some of the straw and dirt to reveal rough wooden planks. She lifts the planks. There's a hole down underneath the root cellar. It's a hole beneath a hole.

"Get inside," Anna says.

I slide through, down to this deep underground hole. The hole is about six and a half feet wide, six and a half feet long. The sides are dirt, the rich, thick black soil these farms are known for. The bottom is dirt, too, packed down tight. Once I am inside, Anna puts back the wooden planks. I can hear her spreading dirt and straw back on top. I am surrounded by dirt with wooden planks for a roof. It's like a dug grave.

There are three other people already hiding in the hole. A young woman in her twenties, a young man who is about 20, and a little girl about four years old. I sit next to the little girl, opposite the woman and the man. The hole is deep enough for me to sit up in, kind of hunched, but too shallow to stand in, and too small for me to stretch out my legs. All our legs touch. They are always touching.

It's dark all the time, except when food is brought at night and a candle is lit. I can smell the dirt, a dark, wet smell that gets caught at the back of my throat. All I know is I am from the town, not from out here in what feels like the middle of nowhere. I am eight years old, wearing my favorite dress, the one my mother made for me. She stitched the delicate flowers and leaves, and they look so beautiful, the vivid blue, burnt orange, and purple flowers cradled by little bursts of bright green leaves jutting out against a white cloth background. The neck is stitched with blue, the color of a cloudless sky. It's too dark to see the colors, except when the candle is lit, but I know they are there.

The other three people are named Rose; her little girl, Betka; and Rose's brother, Abraham. But no one calls him that. They call him Dolo. Even though we are all Jewish and in great danger, they don't like having me here. It means they have to share what little food they are given, what little space they have.

I spend nine months in the hole. I never once take off the dress.

CONTENTS

PART ONE: *THE MARKETPLACE*   1

PART TWO: *THE OTHER SIDE OF THE BRIDGE*   33

PART THREE: *THE BIRDHOUSES*   67

DEDICATIONS AND ACKNOWLEDGMENTS   98

BOOKS AND WEB SITES OF INTEREST   100

PART ONE:
THE MARKETPLACE

CHAPTER ONE ✡

It's a beautiful Sunday afternoon in September 1939, with golden light that makes everything glow. I don't have to wear a coat, and the air is so soft and clean and fresh that I breathe in deeply. Soon it will be cold — I know this. Polish winters can be fierce. That's when I have to get all bundled up and then still feel cold. I am almost five years old and small for my age. I'm with my mother, wearing one of the embroidered dresses she's made for me.

Nearby, there's a magnificent open marketplace, which is right across the street from where I live. It's got columns and graceful archways and long stairs that lead up to several stories with all kinds of shops. It's bright and airy and noisy, and it's where everybody comes to sell what they have to sell — meats, breads, cakes, fruits, flowers, anything you could possibly want. The flowers are amazing, changing through the year — daffodils, tulips, irises, roses, violets, forget-me-nots. Polish people love giving and getting flowers. My favorite flower is the silver thistle. It looks like a silver sunflower and it's surrounded by prickly green leaves. The marketplace, which spans about two city blocks, has a clock tower at one end that chimes on the hour.

The marketplace is the heartbeat of the town, where people gather and exchange news, gossip, information. The town is known for its brilliant Jewish rabbi and scholars, and people come from all over Poland, just to talk. To me, the marketplace is the busy center of the world, and I get to live just opposite it.

I was born October 4, 1934, and I live in the Polish town of Czortków — pronounced "chort-kuv." The "cz" in Polish sounds like "ch," the "ó" sounds like "u," and the "w" sounds like a "v." Czortków is neither a great big city nor a tiny village, but something in between — a big town, an old town. The buildings on one side of the market-place are tall, four and five stories high, which gives Czortków a "city" feel, but it's in a valley surrounded by farmland and on three sides by mountains. Some of the mountains have lush forests, which look bright green in summer and are covered with snow in winter. The Seret River bends its way through town — the river, along with the fresh mountain air, has made Czortków a place to which people come on vacation. They send home postcards show-ing how the spectacular mountains circle and pro-tect the town.

The town has a population of about 40,000 people. Of these, almost half are Poles. They are Catholic. Almost a quarter are Ukrainians, who are Orthodox Christians, and there are about 10,000 Jews. I am Jewish. My last name, Rein, means "clean" in Yiddish and German — clean like the mountain air.

I live with my parents and grandparents — my mother's father and mother. This is not unusual, for the generations to live together, whether the families are Polish or Jewish or Ukrainian. I speak Polish with my parents and Yiddish with my grandparents.

My grandfather is a wonderful tinsmith, a very clever man. He makes the pots and pans that everyone in town uses. His shop is the ground floor of our home. He is handsome with a short, neatly clipped white beard and a long white mustache. He always dresses in black, a somber color, and wears a black hat.

I share a bedroom in the back with my parents. Their double bed is pressed against the wall, and there's a little bed for me. Across from my bed, there's a wardrobe to hold our clothes. The bedroom windows look out onto a low rooftop. To take baths, we pull a bathtub into the kitchen and fill it with water from the sink.

We certainly don't live in luxury, but life is not bad at all! We always have plenty to eat, including chicken and beef twice a day. My grandfather insists on it! Both my grandparents are religious, and my mother keeps a kosher kitchen. A meal can be chicken soup and beef brisket, which is soft and juicy, or cabbage leaves stuffed with meat, and beet soup with a potato in it, or dumplings called pierogis, made with meat or potatoes or both. The kitchen wall is only half wood with glass on top. So, when I'm helping my mother prepare a meal, I can see into my bedroom.

The big meal of the day is lunch, at noon. My father eats lunch with us and always takes a nap in the afternoon before going back to work. He makes mattresses and furniture, and covers chairs with beautiful fabrics. I'm told I look a lot like him. Both of us have thick hair, though he is dark-haired and I am blonde. He has a high forehead, small ears, and gentle eyes. He plays a lot of chess and reads constantly. When he is finished with a book, he closes it with a loud thump, triumphantly. Sometimes I can see dust particles in the light, after the thump.

A corridor separates our apartment from another family's apartment. At the end of the corridor, narrow steps go down into a small open-air courtyard. Because of these steps, the roof behind our bedroom curves down. We can hang bedding out of the bedroom window onto this roof to air out. Behind another low building, on the right, is a storage area that's roofed over. That storage area is boring. It's got old furniture and other leftover stuff. My mother won't let me play there, and anyway, I don't want to, it's so dirty and dusty.

My mother has dark hair that curls around her ears, and bangs, and round cheeks, hooded eyes, and a mischievous smile. She is known, in the family and among her friends, as an exceptionally smart woman. She is industrious, hardworking, her hands always busy — sewing, knitting. She's a talented seamstress. She makes all my clothes, and I love getting new dresses. No one in town makes dresses like hers. When I put on these dresses, I feel like a princess with a fairy godmother!

My grandmother has a face as round as a pie tin. She has a broad, flat nose and a wide smile. She, too, wears mostly dark colors, and, because she is so religious, she wears a wig. I absolutely adore her.

I know nothing of the larger world, only my Czortków world, with its busy marketplace and my close, loving family — parents, grandparents, and assorted aunts and uncles and cousins who live nearby. I feel so safe that I don't even know that I feel safe. It's part of who I am, like my ability to breathe, something I don't have to pay attention to — it's just always there. Every once in a while, someone on the street calls out to someone else, "Dirty Jew." Never to a child, of course. I don't know why they do this and I don't pay much attention to it, anyway.

As my mother and I take a walk that lovely September afternoon, people start to gather in the street. They're not shopping or chatting. They're just standing around, staring. Soon there are hordes of them lining the street on both sides.

"The Russian soldiers are here," my mother tells me.

I see tanks, trucks, and soldiers. They look enormous. But I'm not scared. If anything, it's kind of interesting. I don't know why they are here, but here they are.

Then I hear gunshots.

In that moment, I have one thought: *Life is not going to be the same.*

My mother grabs me, and we run into the front of the nearest building. We can't tell where the shooting is coming from. The sounds echo in all directions. I try to make sense of the sounds, but I can't.

My mother says, "Don't be afraid."

But I'm terrified. I've never known a feeling like this. Before, I got scared if I woke up in the middle of the night after a bad dream. Now, my chest is tight and I can't take in any air. Suddenly, breathing is not automatic. This is our town, our home. It's the middle of the day. It doesn't seem real. It seems too real.

"It'll be all right," my mother tells me.

We stay in the entrance of that building until things quiet down. It's only about 15 or 20 minutes. This is when I realize that a small amount of time can be its own eternity — endless, and beginning-less, too, because suddenly everything that's come before this feels as though its only purpose was to lead me here.

We go home.

People say everyone's first memory is of something terrible. Usually, that means something that's terrible only for you — like falling out of your carriage. This episode, hiding from the shooting, becomes my first memory, something I will carry with me for the rest of my days. My "memory button," so to speak, got turned on that day, September 17, 1939. After this, I remember things vividly. There are gaps, to be sure, but from now on certain things stay in my head, forever.

The Russians take over the town.

Several days later, I'm standing in my grandfather's shop, looking out the window at the marketplace, as I've always loved to do. There's a man,
running beneath the arches. Two Russian soldiers
with rifles yell at him, "Stop! Stop!"

The man raises his arms. But he won't — or
can't — stop running.

"Stop! Stop!" they call again.

He does not stop.

They shoot. I see him fall. I start to scream. My
mother pulls me away from the window. The sound
of my own screaming fills my ears.

CHAPTER TWO ✡

"The Jews are a diseased race."

This is the kind of thing that Adolf Hitler, the chancellor of Germany and head of the Nazi party, keeps telling the world during the 1930s. His words are presented as scientific fact, not opinion: Jews were born into slavery, he says, which makes them inferior by nature. The Germans are the "master race" that must take over the world. In order to do so, the "master race" must destroy the "slave race." Some of his speeches are even broadcast in Czortków, blasted from loudspeakers in the city hall square.

In 1941, although most of the world doesn't yet

know it, Hitler comes up with a plan to execute all of Europe's Jews. He calls it the Final Solution.

The citizens of Germany, many of whom are out of work after the First World War, listen eagerly to Hitler, and many of them blame the Jews for all of the country's misfortunes. Of course, the whole world is in the grip of the Great Depression, and unemployment is a worldwide problem, not just Germany's. Still, Hitler is widely believed when he says that Jews are the cause of all the misery. Hitler hates many groups, such as the Roma people, sometimes called Gypsies, and he deals harshly with anyone who stands up to him, even Christians.

Even before the Final Solution, Hitler begins to rid Germany of its Jews methodically, step by step, as historians now point out.

The first step is to identify who is Jewish. Eventually, Jews have to wear a yellow star sewn to their clothing at all times, and their official papers are marked with a large "J." Next, new laws take away Jewish land and property and make it so that Jews cannot work in certain professions or run their own businesses. Then Jews are physically removed from the rest of the population by placing them into restricted areas called ghettos. From there, they are taken to concentration camps, which hold large numbers, or concentrations, of Jews. This formula, with the same steps, will soon be followed in much of the rest of Europe, too.

In 1938 a German officer is killed in Paris by a Jew. This sets off a backlash that results in the Night of the Broken Glass. On November 9, all over Germany and Austria, which has become part of Germany, Nazis break the windows in synagogues, set them on fire, and smash the windows of Jewish-owned stores. The Nazis say the broken glass looks so beautiful it shines like crystal, which is why this night is called *Kristallnacht* in German. A thousand Jews are killed, and tens of thousands of Jews are sent to concentration camps.

Some Jews leave Germany and Austria. Others, who believe this is only temporary madness, remain where they are.

In the summer of 1939, even though Europe is still at peace, Czortków starts having nightly black-outs. All the streetlights are turned off, and my parents have to tape black paper over the windows. That way, if a German bomber pilot is flying over-head, he won't be able to see us.

On September 1, 1939, Hitler invades Poland, where 3.3 million Jews live, more than in any other country in Europe. England and France declare war on Germany. This is the beginning of the Second World War, which lasts six terrible years.

Just before the war begins, Germany and Russia sign an agreement not to invade each other. A secret part of this pact is a plan to divide Poland between them once the war starts. Now, as far as the world is concerned, there is no more Poland. The western half becomes German, and the eastern half Russian.

My family and I live in the eastern half. That is why the Russian soldiers have marched into Czortków.

At first, many Jews are excited that the Russians have come to protect them from the Nazis. The Poles, who are bitter about losing their freedom, deeply resent the Jews for not hating the Russians. The gunfire I couldn't make sense of when the Russians came to town — that was young Polish men, shooting at the Russian army.

The Russians treat the Poles like second-class citizens, and the Poles grow even more angry —

Jews should be treated this way, not Poles. The Russians send people they don't like — mostly Poles — to Siberia, thousands of miles away in eastern Russia. The Russians are Communists, so there are no more private businesses or private property. Life is hard and there is less food to eat.

My other grandfather, my father's father, can no longer run his small bakery. One day, my father is taken away. We don't know where he is. We think it's somewhere nearby — maybe the nearest big city, Lwów (pronounced "Luh-vuv"). One afternoon my mother says, "I have a feeling, a premonition. I'm going to make dinner for your father. He's coming home tonight."

And he does.

I get sick with pneumonia. I'm so weak, I can't walk. I stay in bed for weeks. I stare up at the ceiling. There is nothing to see. Dr. Knöbel is here all the way from the big city of Kraków, 150 miles away, because Kraków is now under German rule. He hangs dripping-wet sheets in my room. I guess the moisture from the sheets is supposed to help me.

Dr. Knöbel's housekeeper, who has been taking care of his place in Kraków while he is gone, writes to him, "You can come home now. It's safe here." Dr.

Knöbel goes to the Russians to get the proper papers. The Russian police are suspicious. "Why would you want to return to the Germans?" they want to know. They think he's a spy, and he's sent to Siberia, along with his wife and daughter.

My mother feels terrible. She sends them packages, full of food and warm clothing.

Gradually, I get my strength back.

In the spring of 1941, I am six and a half years old. I go to nursery school. My father's cousin runs the school out of her home. There are about a dozen other kids, including my cousin. We put on plays and get all dressed up.

In one play, I am Queen Esther. In ancient Persia, there were a lot of exiled Jews from Israel. Haman, the prime minister of Persia, wanted to kill all the Jews. Esther risked her own life to destroy his plans and save the Jews. Esther's heroics are celebrated on the Jewish holiday of Purim. In the play, I sing a song in Hebrew: "I have a crown upon my head!" I have to hold the crown when I'm singing, so it doesn't fall off.

There are rumors. We know little about what is happening in Germany, or in the German part of Poland, but some people are saying that Jews are already being sent to concentration camps, where conditions are horrid, and then they are killed, or made to work in labor camps until they die of starvation or exhaustion.

People sit by their radios waiting for news, any news. Germany, which by now has taken over Czechoslovakia, Holland, Denmark, Norway, Belgium, and France, as well as Austria and Poland, is going to war with Russia, despite their pact. The Russians will leave our town, and the Germans will take over. Hearing this makes me nervous. I have felt safe under the Russians. Even though I saw a man get shot. At least, there was a reason — he was running, he wouldn't stop. Even though my father was taken away. After all, he came back.

My mother's sister-in-law says to her, "Let's go with the Russians when they leave."

My mother says, "Leave? How can I leave? My life is here. My family. My things."

"Please," my aunt begs her. "I don't want to go alone."

But my mother doesn't want to leave. Her sister-in-law doesn't leave, either. Ninety percent of the Jews in town don't leave.

My father's cousins — three sisters, a brother, and their families — go with the Russians. So, after only six months, that's the end of nursery school for me.

Czortków is silent for several days after the Russians leave. Then the Germans start firing shells at a town bridge. I can hear booming; I feel the walls shake.

The Germans come into town on July 6, 1941, a Sunday, just like the day the Russians got here. I see them arrive, marching with their guns and tanks, wearing goggles, tall black boots, and leather jackets. I understand. This is what invading soldiers do. What I don't understand is what happens among the people in our town.

The three populations in Czortków — the Catholic Poles, the Orthodox Christian Ukrainians, and the Jews — lead mostly separate lives. The Poles speak Polish and write using the Roman alphabet, the way English is written. The Ukrainians, who tend to live in the countryside, speak mostly Ukrainian and use the Cyrillic alphabet in which Russian is written. The Jews, who live in town, speak Polish, except for the religious Jews, who speak Yiddish and use the Hebrew alphabet. What we all wear is different, too. I especially like the way the Ukrainian women dress when they come to town on Sundays, in their long, embroidered white shirts, purple-red skirts, and many-colored belts. They also wear circles of flowers in their hair, with long, dangling ribbons. In Czortków, despite the many differences, when we see one another in the marketplace, everyone is polite.

Because the Russians treated the Poles badly, you might think that the Poles, under German rule, would show hostility to the Jews. But in our town, it's the Ukrainians who change. Now they pick on the Jews. We hear "dirty Jews" constantly — to children, too. Groups of Ukrainian kids attack Jews. One gang beats up my father. I see him afterward. He is all bloody. His clothes are soaked. It is a dark, claylike red. He is never the same after this.

It's not long before my father becomes gravely ill.

"What's wrong with him?" I ask my mother.

She says, "His blood is turning to water."

I don't know what she means.

Food grows even more scarce. My mother tries to get my father some liver, which has iron, to build up his strength, but she can't. He probably needs blood transfusions, but of course they're not available. A local Jewish doctor treats him, but medical supplies are limited.

My father is dying. My mother thinks I don't realize this. But lots of relatives are always stopping by. We live in such close quarters. I hear things. How could I not know? I'm taken to a cousin's house, so I won't see my father die.

My father dies at home in the summer of 1942. It's a warm day. The sun is hot on the back of my neck. I come home from my cousin's house, and my father simply isn't there.

My father's mother dies only a few days after my father — of grief. My mother's father, the gifted tinsmith who liked to eat meat twice a day, is dead, too. He had a stroke right after the German occupation.

I have never in my young life lost anybody. Now I am losing people whom I love. Now I have to take in the concepts of "gone" and "forever." I look to my mother. She's not falling apart. She's staying strong.

For me.

CHAPTER THREE ✡

By April 1942, now that the Germans are here, all the Jews in Czortków are confined to a ghetto, a series of streets and buildings where Jews must live. Unless you have the right papers, you cannot leave the ghetto. My mother has working papers, so she can come and go. Because she is so good at sewing, the Germans have made her take a job fixing their uniforms. If you are found outside the ghetto without the proper papers, you are killed on the spot.

As it happens, we are still in our home. Our house is right on the border of the ghetto, so we don't have to move. I can still see the wonderful marketplace, hear the clock chime on the hour, but I can't go there anymore; only Poles and Ukrainians can. We are completely cut off from the other communities, except from the Ukrainian farmers from the countryside who, if they are careful, come over the bridge at the edge of town, and, at the edge of the ghetto, sell us their fruits, vegetables, milk, and cheese.

We don't know it yet (because the Germans don't explain things, they just do them), but we are being forced to live the steps that Hitler created for dealing with the Jews. So far, we have been identified as Jews, must wear armbands with Jewish stars, and we have been confined to the ghetto. Now we are starting to be taken away.

On Wednesday, August 26, and in the early hours of Thursday, August 27, comes the first "action." It's a word that could have many meanings, but for the Germans it means only one thing: a day set aside for rounding up huge numbers of Jews and putting them on trains headed for concentration camps.

About half a dozen of our neighbors find a place to hide. There's a windowless room that kind of sticks out into the next-door storage area I'm not allowed to play in. You get to this room through a door from an apartment. Our neighbors run in there. Someone pulls a wardrobe in front of the door to conceal it.

We, too, are heading for this room.

At the last moment, my mother changes her mind. She swerves aside and takes me and my grandmother over to the back wall of the main storage area. She pulls away a board down near the floor. What is she doing? How does she even know to do this? "Crawl in," she says.

My grandmother and I have to turn around backward, facing away from the wall, lie down on the floor, slide on our backs under the wall, and then kind of shimmy upright again, so that we are standing on the other side of the wall. We are in a long but incredibly narrow space between the storage-area wall and the wall of another apartment building next door. My mother comes in last and puts the board back, so we can't be seen. There's so little room that all we can do is stand there, facing front, shoulder to shoulder. We can't even move.

Suddenly, the whole idea of "place" changes for me. This space behind the wall isn't just a nothing space. This space has a purpose. It has become the most important space in the world. It can save our lives — if we're not discovered.

The wall is so close I can feel my own warm breath coming back at me. I can't move, but I can see. There are cracks in the boards right in front of me. Because it's in back of the house, instead of plaster over the wall, it's constructed with mud and straw, a rough finish. There's a musty, old smell. We hear police going from door to door, trying to find Jews. We can hear children crying, dogs barking, shooting, glass breaking, Ukrainian policemen yelling "dirty Jew." It's loud and chaotic.

We stand there for hours. That night, Ukrainian policemen come into the building. They start banging on the walls. I can see mud slip down through the cracks. The policemen notice the little room that sticks out into the storage area. They go into the apartment behind it to investigate. They are ruthlessly thorough. They see that a wardrobe has been moved and that it's blocking a door. They push the wardrobe aside and find our neighbors in the room we almost hid in.

I see our neighbors getting taken away. One of them points right to the spot where we are standing behind the wall.

"There are Jews hiding in there, too," he says.

"Let's look," a policeman says.

I can't believe what I'm hearing. It's bad enough that the Ukrainians, our neighbors for years and years, have turned on us. But a Jew turning on other Jews? It doesn't make sense. It's as if the sky is suddenly below our feet and the ground is over our heads. It's wrong. It's backward.

I want to scream. I almost scream.

My mother puts her hand on my mouth. She warns me with her eyes. *Do not make a sound.*

The police bang on the wall, inches from us. Mud and straw fall on their uniforms. The policemen look disgusted. One of them says to another, "Ah, there are no Jews back there. That Jew just wanted us to work extra. Let's go."

They leave.

We stay behind the wall all night, until it's quiet. Finally, the "action" ends.

Slowly, slowly, you come out of your hiding place.

Then you look for your family.

My aunt, the one who wanted to go to Russia but didn't, is gone, taken away, with her husband and two daughters. Another aunt and her little girl

are gone, too. Another aunt and her two sons —
gone. In one day and night, 2,000 Jews have disap-
peared, vanished.

My family is now only me, my mother, my
grandmother, two uncles who were taken away by
the Russian army, and an uncle who was sent to a
work camp. Who can say if the uncles in the
Russian army are alive or dead? How long will my
other uncle last in the work camp? What if a policeman decides to test his aim and shoots him?

After this first "action," the ghetto is
"reduced" — shrunken, so the remaining Jews are
crammed into even fewer buildings. Our building
is still inside the smaller ghetto, so we still don't
have to move.

In the days that follow, there are other, smaller
"actions." We go to our little hiding place again.

Now it's Purim, March 21, 1943. Purim, the day
that celebrates Queen Esther. Purim is always a
happy holiday. It's kind of the Jewish Halloween —
kids dress up and have fun.

On her way to work this Purim, outside the
marketplace, my mother, along with a cousin and

two other women, are stopped by the head of the German police, walking his dog. German police are the Gestapo. My mother has her papers with her. She shows him her papers. It's cold and windy.

His name is Kurt Köllner. He decides — I don't know what he decides. Some witnesses hear him say something about how another Gestapo policeman has come into his territory — "he shot my Jews" — and now Köllner wants to "shoot his Jews."

He takes the four women from the marketplace to the prison courtyard.

He orders them to take off all their clothes.

They stand there shivering.

He shoots them all dead.

Meanwhile, I'm behind my building, playing. I'm eight years old.

People start asking me where they can find Ekka. That is my grandmother's nickname, based on her name, Esther.

What's going on? I'm wondering. *Why are so many people looking for my grandmother?*

I go inside to see what's happening.

I always call my grandmother *Babcia*, which is Polish for "grandmother." It's pronounced "Bab-cha."

"Babcia, what is it?" I ask her.

"Something very bad has happened to your mother," she tells me, in a low, gentle voice. "Your mother was shot."

I hear the words.

Then she says, "I'll take care of you."

And, "I want you to remember always. When you live to survive this war, you will light a candle for your mother every Purim."

I hear these words, too. I am listening carefully. I realize she has said something very important. What she said was, "*When* you live to survive this war." She did not say "If." It's like she's giving me her blessing, her guarantee, her solemn oath. She is looking ahead. I will live out this war. I will live for many years beyond the war, to see many Purims. On each of these Purims, I will light a candle for my mother.

I think about how Babcia handles loss. She had six children. One died in infancy. We don't know the fate of the two sons in the Russian army. She has lost three other children, two sons and a daughter, to the war — her daughter just this morning.

What does Babcia do now?

She puts all her energy into saving me.

One evening, a few months after my mother has been killed, Babcia takes me aside just as I'm about to go to bed. She says, "You cannot go to sleep. Tonight you will sneak out of the ghetto."

"Sneak out — where?" I say.

"I have arranged for a Ukrainian woman to be waiting for you under the bridge. You will go with her."

I can't believe what I'm hearing. I'm leaving — tonight? The bridge is outside the ghetto. Why am I going to the bridge?

"You have to be careful as you walk to the bridge," Babcia says. "Stay close to the buildings. If you hear a noise, stop and hide until it's quiet again."

I start to cry.

"You can't do that," she says. "You have to be strong."

She also says, "I'll be thinking of you."

And, "I'll be here for you."

And, "Don't forget to be a good girl."

She gives me a little bundle with some clothes. And a tin cup. My grandfather made the cup.

"This is a special cup," she says. "It has a double bottom. You see?"

She shows me how to unscrew the bottom. It's magical, like something in a fairy tale. A cup with a secret hiding place.

"There's money in it," she says. "If you ever need money — and you may need it to save your life — it's in there. Don't ever part with it. Promise me."

"I promise."

I understand what's going on. I'm old enough. But Babcia is all I have. "You'll come with me, won't you?" I ask.

"No," she says.

"But — at least to the bridge?"

"No. You will go alone."

PART TWO:
THE OTHER SIDE OF THE BRIDGE

CHAPTER FOUR ✡

Once the war begins, borders all over Europe close and Jews cannot leave their countries. In each of these countries, Jewish parents are looking ahead, desperately trying to find ways to keep their children safe until the war ends. Jewish children are especially vulnerable, because Hitler wants to be sure to erase future generations. Parents have to decide whether to keep their children with them, or hand them over to non-Jews willing to hide them. Often, children are given to complete strangers.

Hiding children, it turns out, is easier than hiding adults. Children do not have to have papers.

Children can simply show up on a farm as some-body's cousin's child whose parents are dead or ill. Or they can be placed in an orphanage or in a convent. One historian later calls these the "visible" ways of hiding. Visible children are hidden in plain sight. But they have to keep their true identities secret: their accents, their native language, and above all, the fact that they are Jewish. There are always people, even other children, looking for Jews in hiding. When you turn in Jews, sometimes there's a reward — money, a little coffee, or sugar. Much of the time, people turn in Jews for no reward at all.

How and where a child will be hidden depends on whom the parents know, whom they can trust, and how much they can afford to pay. You don't know in advance who might help you. Some people who say terrible things about Jews take Jewish children into their homes, anyway. Others, who hate Hitler and everything he stands for, say no, because they are too afraid they will be caught and punished.

Arrangements are made in the strictest secrecy. If someone hears that someone else's little girl is going to be hidden, he might try to set it up so that his own little girl takes her place and goes into hiding instead. At any time, of course, things can go wrong. My grandmother must have been planning my hiding for weeks, probably ever since my mother died — finding someone she could trust, and a safe place, and paying them for it. But Babcia had not said a word to me.

The risks to people who hide Jewish children are enormous. On October 15, 1941, the Germans made a law that anyone providing shelter to Jews, or giving them food, or even selling them food, is to be killed. Poland is the only occupied country with this automatic death penalty. And it isn't just the helpers who are in terrible danger. When Polish people are caught helping Jews, their entire families and even their neighbors are killed, too. In one village, some people give food to 100 Jews hidden in a forest. When the Germans find out, they burn down the entire village with everyone still inside their homes.

I don't want to go. I can't bear to leave Babcia. But I go.

I walk quietly and carefully. I stay close to the buildings, as Babcia told me to. I'm so close, the walls sometimes brush against my coat. I keep looking behind me. I am quiet — so quiet that I can't hear my own footsteps. I see no one at all.

Under the bridge, there's a lot of brush. I sit down. It's a cool evening. The leaves are prickly against the back of my neck.

I wait.

After a few minutes, I hear footsteps and the swishing of a skirt. I know that Ukrainian women wear long skirts that make this rustling sound. But what if I'm hearing it wrong? What if the person coming toward me is a policeman on patrol? I could be shot.

I step out of the brush.

I see a woman wearing a kerchief.

"I came for you," she says to me in Polish. "You will be staying with me for a while."

I nod at her.

"Follow me."

I pick up my bundle, and we cross the Seret River on the narrow bridge, which has tall cast-iron girders that crisscross one another. I can walk on the bridge openly. I'm no longer a child wandering out alone after midnight — now I'm with a Ukrainian woman. I could be her child. That feels safe. But I'm still afraid, my heart beating wildly. If we should be stopped, I don't speak Ukrainian, and the police are Ukrainian. If you don't speak Ukrainian, you are assumed to be Jewish, simple as that.

We walk for quite a while, maybe two miles, before we get to her home. It's still dark, before sunrise. Czortków seems far behind us. I don't know this area at all. The woman's name is Tekla Zacharczuk. She has a farm with a straw-thatched roof, where she lives with her daughter and son-in-law. Inside the house, there's a long hallway. To the left is a big living room. At the back of the living room, there's an archway with a curtain. And there's a narrow, little room behind the curtain, only as wide as a bed.

"You have to stay in that room," Tekla tells me. "When the dog barks, crawl under the bed."

I do as she says. I am not forgetting to be a good girl, as Babcia instructed me.

Tekla's son-in-law resents that I'm here. "She's just a dirty little Jew," he says. "She'll get us into trouble. We'll suffer because of her!"

I can go to the bathroom early in the morning and at night. If I have to go during the day, I'm not allowed. I have to hold it and hold it. There's a window, but it's too high for me to stand up and reach. That's probably good, because I might be tempted to look outside and then someone might see me.

I once heard about an animal in the Polish forests called a marmot — a kind of ground squirrel, a member of the beaver family, about as big as a cat. When marmots are scared or angry, they make a whistling sound. I'm not out in a deep forest, full of oak and beech trees. I'm on a farm with fields and cows and chickens. But I wonder if I can hear the marmots whistle if I listen hard enough.

I have absolutely nothing else to do.

I stare at the blank walls. I remember how bored I felt when I had pneumonia. That was so much better than this. It's spring 1943, still windy and cold. The woman's son-in-law works in the fields. I'm always scared of him.

That's the life of the child in hiding: being bored and being scared.

I never hear a marmot whistle, but when the dog barks, I rush under the bed.

The Ukrainians are a superstitious people. They believe there are spirits everywhere — in the trees and fields and rivers. There are dangers at almost every turn, and to avoid them you have to be aware of omens. If the chickens get sick, that's a bad sign. You never bring an even number of flowers to someone's house. It means death will come to the home. You don't leave an empty bottle on a table. It will bring disaster. During Christmas, you put an ax outside your door to keep away evil spirits. If a woman gives a man an Easter egg that is undecorated on top, he will lose all his hair. If you whistle indoors, you will lose all your money. Before you go on a journey, sit on your luggage. This will ward off bad luck while traveling. After someone dies, family members and friends gather at the grave nine days after the death, and forty days after, and one year after. This is when the spirit is nearby. Candles are lit and a meal is eaten next to the grave. A glass of vodka is left so the spirit can drink from it.

The worst thing of all is the evil eye.

If someone gives you the evil eye, terrible things will happen to you. You will lose your money. You will get sick. You will die. Some people wear mirrors beneath their clothes, to reflect the evil eye back to the person sending it.

I don't call it the evil eye. I've never seen the evil eye. I don't even know what it means. I do know that there is someone in the house with me, under the same roof, someone with two eyes who wishes I would disappear. That son-in-law. I am as invisible as I can possibly be. It's not enough. He wants me dead.

Sometimes I'm allowed in the big living room, when it's safe and no one's around. One night, about two months after I arrive, a man and a woman simply walk into that room when I'm there. The dog isn't barking. These people must not be strangers to the household.

The man starts to talk to me.

I'm stunned for a moment. Somehow — I don't know how — I come up with an idea. It's like I grow up in that instant. I have to. And something inside me knows what to do, the way my mother knew to pull the board away from the wall.

I point to my ears, like I'm deaf. I point to my mouth, like I can't talk.

Tekla, who is watching, picks up on this. "She's a deaf-mute," she tells the couple. "She's a distant relative, only here for the night. I'm taking her back home tomorrow."

The man and the woman leave me alone.

After this, the son-in-law carries on something awful. "That's it," he says. "I'm taking her to the Gestapo tomorrow."

Sometime in the night, I feel someone shaking me. Is it the son-in-law, coming to take me to the Gestapo? No, it's Tekla. She has a finger to her mouth. *Don't speak*. Then she whispers to me, "Get dressed. We're going someplace."

I put on my favorite dress, the white one my mother made, with flowers and leaves. I take nothing with me. I'm so scared, I don't even take the special cup. The cup I promised Babcia I would keep with me always.

We don't walk on roads. We walk through fields. Tekla's walking ahead so quickly, I have to run to keep up with her. It's June, but cool at night — why didn't I bring my coat? I try to keep my thoughts in order. I'm so terrified, it's not easy. I don't even know what direction we're heading in. Are we going to the Gestapo? No, not likely. She wouldn't take me at night, when they're asleep. Maybe she's taking me back to the ghetto, back to my grandmother. That would be heaven!

We reach another farmhouse. Later I find out we're near Czortków, on the outskirts of town, in an area called Vignanka. This is where my nursery school was. At the moment, it doesn't feel at all familiar.

The house belongs to Tekla's sister. Her name is Anna Aksenczuk. Anna is in a barn, waiting for us. She is short, with small, narrow eyes, dark hair, thin lips, round pale cheeks, and a scarf tied tightly around her face so it looks like a perfect circle, like the full moon.

CHAPTER FIVE ✡

Inside the barn, next to the wooden wall, is a trap-door that leads down to a root cellar with brick walls. There are bins for potatoes and a dirt floor with straw on it. Anna pushes aside some of the straw and dirt to reveal rough wooden planks. She lifts the planks. There's a hole down underneath the root cellar. It's a hole beneath a hole.

"Get inside," Anna says.

I slide through, down to this deep underground hole. The hole is about six and a half feet wide, six and a half feet long. The sides are dirt, the rich, thick black soil these farms are known for. The bottom is dirt, too, packed down tight. Once I am inside, Anna puts back the wooden planks. I can hear her spreading dirt and straw back on top. I am surrounded by dirt with wooden planks for a roof. It's like a dug grave.

There are three other people already hiding in the hole. A young woman in her twenties, a young man who is about 20, and a little girl about four years old. I sit next to the little girl, opposite the woman and the man. The hole is deep enough for me to sit up in, kind of hunched, but too shallow to stand in, and too small for me to stretch out my legs. All our legs touch. They are always touching.

It's dark all the time, except when food is brought at night and a candle is lit. I can smell the dirt, a dark, wet smell that gets caught at the back of my throat. All I know is I am from the town, not from out here in what feels like the middle of nowhere. I am eight years old, wearing my favorite dress, the one my mother made for me. She stitched the delicate flowers and leaves, and they look so beautiful, the vivid blue, burnt orange, and purple flowers cradled by little bursts of bright green leaves jutting out against a white cloth background. The neck is stitched with blue, the color of a cloudless sky. It's too dark to see the colors, except when the candle is lit, but I know they are there.

The other three people are named Rose; her little girl, Betka; and Rose's brother, Abraham. But no one calls him that. They call him Dolo. Even though we are all Jewish and in great danger, they don't like having me here. It means they have to share what little food they are given, what little space they have.

I spend nine months in the hole. I never once take off the dress.

I am now one of the "invisible" hidden children.

Some invisible Jewish children are concealed behind double walls, like larger versions of my tin cup. Some lie flat above false ceilings. Attic and cellar doors are disguised, so they don't look like doors anymore. There are children in empty offices and factories, horse stables, pigsties, hay lofts, greenhouses, chicken coops, caves, forest huts, chimneys, sewers, garbage pails. Some of them are in city buildings. If there's an air raid, they can't leave and get to a bomb shelter. Like me, some of them cannot stand up. Like me, they may not know when it is day or night, and never sleep deeply or for long. They sleep a kind of twilight, dreamless sleep.

I learn that Rose's husband is dead, killed in the war. Rose knows Anna because Anna used to sell milk, cheese, and vegetables in the ghetto. One day, when Rose bought green beans from her, Anna told her, "If you're ever in bad trouble, if things get close to very dangerous, come to me, rush to me, and I will hide you at my home."

Anna is not getting money to protect us, unlike her sister. Anna is scared to death that we will be discovered, but she is hiding us, anyway. I don't know why she is doing this. There must be something inside her that is telling her it is the right thing to do.

Anna has two sons. The younger son, who's 10, is named Bohdan (pronounced Bog-dan). He helped Dolo, Rose's brother, dig the hole a couple of weeks before I got there. Bohdan's the one who clears away the straw and removes the wooden planks to bring us food. Potato soup, a little milk, some bread. No meat, of course, ever. Bohdan also empties the bucket at night, the bucket we use to go to the bathroom. But we don't use the bucket much. When you eat so little, you rarely need to go. I'm not the only one who doesn't change clothes. Sometimes we rinse our hands and faces in some cold water. That's all.

Anna's older son is second-in-command of the Ukrainian police. He comes to the house at least once a week. He does not know his mother is hiding Jews. If he finds out, he will kill us himself. When he is around — and you never know when he will come for a visit — Bohdan cannot bring us food. Sometimes the older son stays over for two or three days. In all this time, we don't eat.

It turns out Dolo knows who I am, remembers seeing me around. He used to take Hebrew lessons from a man who lived in the apartment across the corridor from mine. I don't recognize him. He is a stranger. So is Rose. So is her little daughter.

To make money, Anna rents out space in the farmhouse to students from Czortków. Sometimes the students come over to the barn to relax, lean against the outside wall, read, or talk to other students. We must be extra quiet, so the students won't hear us. If we speak at all, it's in whispers.

Mostly, we don't speak. Rose, her brother, her daughter — they have nothing to say to me. I have nothing to say to them. It's like I am becoming the deaf-mute I was pretending to be. Rose — the name doesn't suit her. She is nothing like a flower. She is hard and cold. I have never felt quite this terrible. I remember how upset I used to be, back in that narrow, little farmhouse room, alone. But what kind of life is this? Children are supposed to be noisy, not silent. They are supposed to run around, not remain in one spot, all cramped up. They are supposed to feel the sunshine, not have the floor of a root cellar for a roof. They are supposed to be part of the world, not live like they don't exist. They are supposed to be with their loving families, not buried alive with people who could care less about her.

Sometimes Vignanka, the area around Anna's farm, is searched for Jews. Twice the police come and search her house, but not the barn. Anna is so terrified after the first search that she is sick for three months and has to stay in bed. During this time, she makes sure that Bohdan takes care of us.

I get lice. I feel like I'm on fire, they itch so badly. Rose asks Anna for a pair of scissors, and she cuts off all my hair, right down to the scalp. I'm so upset about this. I have such beautiful hair! Now my head feels like stiff, little bristles. Rose has to cut off her little girl's hair, too. We're all infested. The lice crawl on my face. They live in the seams of my dress. I pick the nits — the lice eggs — out of my dress and crack them apart with my thumbnails. They make a little bursting sound that is, strangely, satisfying. *I got that one!* I think with triumph. I snap open thousands of them.

As the months pass, it grows cold and damp. Why didn't I bring my coat? Anna gives us blankets, but they are never warm enough. The temperature can go below zero, and the earth feels like ice.

I'm frightened always — so frightened it is now an automatic part of me, the way breathing used to be. Cold always. Hungry always. I kind of shut down and go numb. If I have any thoughts at all, they are with my grandmother. *She's waiting for me. She's still alive. She has to be! Otherwise, I'll be alone. What'll I do then?*

Just after the new year of 1944, Anna tells us that the Germans are losing the war and retreating. In March, we hear fighting nearby — tanks rumbling, the crack of gunfire. This time for me it's a wonderful sound. Anna tells us we are now free — "liberated" by the Russians, she says. But Anna doesn't want us to leave her farm during the day. Even with the Germans gone, she is terrified that her neighbors will find out she's been hiding Jews.

One morning in March 1944, before sunrise, we crawl out of the hole.

CHAPTER SIX ✡

All four of us walk to town. There's snow on the ground. It's cold. After sitting for so long in the hole, my legs don't work right. They're stiff, not bending properly. They feel like doll legs. My shoes are so tight now, and my toes hurt.

It surprises me when we reach Czortków — have we really been that close to home all this time? We find an empty building where Jews are gathering. It was Gestapo headquarters, and of course all the Germans have fled. Now the Russians control the town, which was officially liberated on March 23.

This building ... it's near the prison compound where my mother was shot.

I must see my grandmother.

Rose tells me that there was a final "action," in late June of last year. The ghetto was "liquidated," and all the Jews were killed. No more ghetto. No more Jews. The Germans declared the town *Judenrein*. This word, *Judenrein*, has my last name, *Rein*, in it, a name that means "clean." So, Czortków has been declared "clean" of Jews. After this, if any Jews were found, they were killed on the spot. If the Gestapo thought Jews were hiding in a building, they burned down the building. Somehow, 100 Jews found safe places to hide. But only 100. Out of Czortków's 10,000 Jews, only 100 are still alive — only one percent.

"Your grandmother's not one of them," Rose says.

"What do you mean?" I say. But I know what she means.

"Your grandmother is dead," she says.

I'm stunned. The one person I had left is gone. The final "action" was already so long ago. My grandmother — she's been dead since I was back in Tekla's farmhouse, even. All this time, all those months in the hole, all the times I thought of her, my grandmother was already dead. I feel ... completely empty. What's the emptiest thing you can think of? A hole. Well, I was in a dark hole, but this feels far more empty than that.

Rose finds that some distant relatives of mine are among the 100 Czortków survivors. She says I must go to them and takes me to their apartment. It's a man, his wife, and their son, who's a little older than me. They give me something to eat, some bread, a little milk. I take a bath — my first in a year. I put on the dress again. I have nothing else to wear. My mother's beautiful embroidery is intact. Inside myself, I feel like 100 years have gone by. But the dress, amazingly, looks almost new.

"Now, you must go back to Rose," my relatives tell me.

Rose is still at Gestapo headquarters, in a small room. She talks to other people in the building and finds a brother-in-law of one of my uncles. He has also survived. He takes me to a house that belonged to another uncle, who was taken to a work camp and didn't survive. But other people, strangers, Poles, are living in the house now.

"Will you take her?" he asks them.

"No," they say.

So I have to go back to Rose.

Meanwhile, there are rumors. The Germans, we hear, are determined to reclaim the territory the Russians have taken. The Nazis may be coming back. So the Jews can't stay; they have to leave Czortków quickly. In fact, shortly after this, the Germans do return for several days; it's only in the summer of 1944 that the Germans completely disappear.

Rose has decided to escape the Germans by returning to Anna's farmhouse. She doesn't want me with her. But she doesn't tell me this. Instead, she takes me to the window. She points to the road. There's a huge march of people, heading east for what was, before the war, land where Poland ended and Russia started, maybe 50 miles away. I've never seen so many people hurrying like that.

"Do you see that?" Rose asks me.

"Yes," I say.

"You have to go with them."

She puts her hands on my shoulders. She walks me to the door. She pushes me out the door and closes the door behind me.

Rose has thrown me out. Now I am even more alone. In the midst of people. I think, *my cousins are better off than I am*. My cousins, of course, are dead.

I walk along the road. It's dark now, getting colder. The ground is full of snow and mud. I'm hungry. I'm shivering. Am I shivering from the cold, or from panic? I have no idea what I'm doing, where I'm going, how I will ever get there or even find something to eat or a place to sleep.

I'm nine and a half years old. My grandmother is dead.

I pass out on the road.

When I wake up, someone is carrying me. A man. I'm on his back, piggy-back style. My dress feels wet, almost icy, because I was lying in the snow. If this man didn't pick me up, I would have frozen to death.

We're still on the road, and we come to a house. The man stops, lets me down gently. He, too, is undernourished and weak, and can't carry me anymore.

"I know who you are," he tells me. "I knew your father."

He goes to the door. "I'm leaving this girl with you," he tells the people inside. "If you don't take care of her, I'll come back and shoot you."

At that moment, some Russian soldiers also approach the house. One of them is a captain.

We go inside the house. The man explains to the captain what's going on.

"Don't worry," the captain says. "We'll take her."

So off I go with the Russian soldiers!

We stop in a town, Dzymalów, not far away.

The soldiers give me a cot, and a little soup, and some bread. But after a few days, the soldiers have orders to move on. Despite the threat to Czortków, the Germans are still very much in retreat. The Russian soldiers are like a huge wave, pushing back the German army, and they have to go wherever the Germans are at the moment.

So here I am, by myself again, this time in the streets of a strange town.

There's a large government building. A whole group from Czortków is inside. I find my uncle's brother-in-law. "Have you anything to eat?" I ask him.

"No," he says. "Just go knock on some doors, and someone will give you some food."

He is telling me I have to beg. This seems unbelievable to me. I can't see myself doing such a thing, going up to strange people's houses and asking for food.

For a long time, I just walk, trying to work up my courage.

There is something about this that is even worse than passing out on the road. I have never before felt so lost.

Finally, I knock on a door. "I'm hungry," I say. "Do you have a piece of bread?"

A woman gives me some milk and a piece of bread.

I spend a few days like this.

Inside the government building, the stairs are wide, like in a school hallway. At night, I can lie down on the steps. They are hard and cold. But that's where I sleep. I have to be careful not to roll over onto the steps below.

One afternoon, a Russian soldier in a truck sees me sitting on some steps in front of the building. "What's going on with you?" he asks me.

I tell him I'm alone.

"I'll take you to an orphanage in Kiev," he says. "Meet me here tomorrow morning, at this exact spot."

Early the next morning, I am there, standing in the doorway. I don't dare sit down, even. I have to be able to see him.

He comes for me.

I sit in the back of his truck. It's like being in a tent. Thick dark-green canvas on poles makes a roof and walls, but when I look toward town, it's open air, and I can see what we're leaving behind.

We drive for several hours. We cross the border that all the people from Czortków were trying to reach. Now there's nothing really there, because the Russians already control the land on both sides of the old line.

We drive for half a day more. The soldier gives me some bread.

And I'm still in that dress!

CHAPTER SEVEN ✡

We stop in a small village — Gritsev. It's not far from a big town, Shebetovka. The sky over Shebetovka is all lit up because the Germans are bombing it. They're retreating from the Russians and bombing it, anyway.

The soldier takes me to the mayor of Gritsev.

"I was about to take this little girl to an orphanage in Kiev," the soldier tells the mayor. "But my plans have changed, and I have to turn around and go back west. I can't take her now."

Another man is also in the mayor's office. He is listening.

"Where are you from?" the mayor asks me.

"Czortków," I tell him.

The other man stands up. He's so short!

His name is Sergei. He is Russian and Jewish and he was a partisan, an underground fighter against the Germans. He lost his wife and children to the war and now he is remarried to a Jewish woman named Dora, who was also a partisan. She has two daughters in their early teens.

"I'll take this girl," Sergei says. "She can live with me. She can be like a little sister to my two daughters."

I live with this family in Gritsev for more than a year. Sergei, Dora, and their daughters are good to me, never cruel. I sleep on a little cot in the living room. It's not like houses in America, where children have their own bedrooms. The little brick houses in Gritsev — which have beautiful geometric patterns of many-colored bricks around the windows, doors, and corners — have only two or three rooms altogether. The daughters sleep in the one bedroom, with their parents.

There's a Ukrainian woman who does housework. I sit and talk with her in the late afternoons.

She reminds me of Babcia. Her name is Martocha. I'm most comfortable with her.

I go to school. I learn the Russian alphabet.

The town's judge, who lives a couple of houses away, gives Dora some material to make me a dress. The new dress is lovely.

So, all is well?

No, this is not a happy ending. My feelings find no rest.

Maybe all the sadness of the last five years is catching up with me. Maybe I am mourning my grandmother, my mother, and everyone else that I lost. Maybe it's other things, too. Back in the hole was never really safe, and always terrifying. But the months passed, and we weren't discovered. We weren't out in the open. We always knew exactly what to do — stay still.

Then we were liberated. Rose could have been kind. Instead she threw me out into the open, where I got handed from one stranger to another, with no idea of what to expect or what could happen. *Don't forget to be a good girl*, Babcia had said. I haven't forgotten. But no matter how good I am, how long will these people keep me?

There are worse things than being hidden, I realize.

I turn 10 years old in Sergei's house. I don't grow much. Probably I will remain short my entire life, I think. I am a quiet, shy girl. In some way, I know that this is not the personality I am supposed to have. I'm so dazed all the time, I barely feel alive. At night, I cry. Quietly, so no one will hear me. If I get a headache or stomachache, I don't go to Sergei and Dora and say, "I'm not feeling well."

This is not my real home. This is not my real family.

Sergei's been writing letters to Czortków. He finds a Jewish woman who knew my mother. She writes that one of my mother's brothers survived — the younger one, George, who had been taken by the Russian army. His wife and child did not survive. My uncle, she tells Sergei, lives in Lwów. The woman says that, if I come to her, she can help me find him.

During this past year, Uncle George (his Hebrew name is Gedalia) has gotten remarried to a Russian woman. One afternoon, on the street, Uncle George bumps into a man from Czortków — people are always looking for news, for a chance of putting something back together, so they ask questions of anyone who looks familiar.

"I think your sister's little daughter survived," the man tells Uncle George.

Uncle George immediately goes to Kiev to look in orphanages for me. He is supposed to have papers to travel, but he goes without papers. Naturally, he can't find me in the orphanages. The police stop Uncle George. Without papers, he's arrested and thrown in jail, where he gets sick — dysentery. That's a bad infection of the intestines that gives you terrible and sometimes life-threatening diarrhea. He writes to his wife, who sends him money. You can — with money — get out of jail.

He goes back home, to Lwów, and regains his health. His wife has meanwhile given birth to a little girl. By this time, Sergei is writing from Gritsev to the woman in Czortków. Uncle George can get papers now, but only to go to Kraków, so he goes there and pays a friend to go to Gritsev and get me.

I know nothing about this. All I know is that I am ready to go to the train station with Sergei, to get on a train for Czortków. The plan is to go back to Czortków to meet the lady who will help me find my uncle. Just as we're heading out the door, in walks a man in a sailor's uniform, with a letter from Uncle George. If Sergei and I had left for the train ten minutes earlier, we would have missed him.

The sailor says his name is Romek Kopyt. Actually, I don't think he's really a sailor. But these days it's probably easier to get past policemen in a sailor's uniform.

I go with Romek to Lwów. Romek, like Sergei, also has a wife named Dora. They don't have any children. I stay with them for several weeks.

In September 1945, I am almost eleven years old. I get on a train again. Romek is taking me to Kraków so I can live with my Uncle George from now on. As soon as we pull into Kraków, I see my uncle. I recognize him. I know him. It's an emotional moment, but I don't cry. I'm beyond tears. There are feelings beyond tears. I meet my new aunt for the first time. I hold their little girl in my arms. She is adorable, six months old.

She is named Ethel, in memory of Esther, my Babcia.

PART THREE:
THE BIRDHOUSES

CHAPTER EIGHT ✡

The Second World War is over — in Kraków, and throughout the world, and for everyone. My baby cousin Ethel will never have to know it or remember it. I think of this amazing fact every time I pick her up.

The war had a lot of different starting and ending points, depending on where you were. For Americans, the war didn't even begin until the day the Japanese, who were on the side of the Germans, bombed Pearl Harbor in Hawaii — December 7, 1941. The Americans then teamed up with the British, the Russians, and the Australians, to form the Allies. These Allies fought the Axis powers —

the Germans, the Japanese, and the Italians. Over time, many more countries joined the Allies. This is what brought the whole world into it.

For years, the Americans were busy pushing the Japanese back across the Pacific Ocean and helping the British push the Germans out of North Africa. Then, on June 6, 1944, American and British soldiers landed in France, to the west of Germany. By this point, the Russians, fighting east of Germany, had already freed Poland, but June 6 — known as D-day — is the day Americans think of as the beginning of the end of the war in Europe.

After D-day, the Russians kept pushing the German army west, while the Allies, advancing through France, kept pushing the Germans east. Eventually they met up, right in the middle of Germany. Adolf Hitler committed suicide, and a week later, on May 7, 1945, Germany surrendered. This is V-E day, "Victory in Europe Day."

But the war wasn't over yet, because the Japanese continued fighting. In early August, America dropped atomic bombs on two Japanese cities. Five days later, Japan also surrendered. This day, August 14, 1945, is V-J day, "Victory over Japan Day."

Despite all this wonderful news, for many people "peace" does not equal "safe." In Poland, Poles are still killing Jews. Some Poles moved into Jewish people's homes when the Germans came and don't want to give them back. The Ukrainians, too, are still killing Jews.

Can you imagine, I think, *going through all you have gone through, and now you are free, and then you are killed by a Pole or a Ukrainian, who may have been your neighbor at one time?* Even today, what they did still makes me angry.

Yet it was a Ukrainian woman, someone I never knew and barely ever saw, who risked everything to save my life.

With Uncle George in Kraków, I'm happy again.

We live in an apartment that is shared by three families. Each family gets one or two rooms, and everyone shares the kitchen. Having a couple of other families around, I feel safe — there's always someone home with me. It's almost fall, getting chilly. My aunt takes me to buy a coat. A new coat — wonderful, just wonderful. Uncle George, who makes the tops of leather boots for a living, makes me a new pair of boots. I am warm all winter, indoors and out. There's food. I eat rolls with cold cuts. Without stopping! I don't know how many I eat, just one after the other. I sit by my uncle's radio and discover Russian songs. I love them — they are sad but full of energy, which makes them not so sad. I sing along with the radio for hours, as loud as I can.

Another girl lives in the apartment, too, Rose Sirato, also called Rosa. She's about my age. She becomes my first real friend. Her father died in the war, and her mother then married Rosa's uncle. There's a school to go to, for Jewish children only, that a Jewish organization has set up in a government building. I sign up for school, and so does Rosa, and we can go to school together.

I like Kraków. I like walking along the streets, seeing the city. It's full of activity. Rynek Główny — the main market square — reminds me of the marketplace back home, except that this one is enormous. All of Czortków could fit into this one space! The tower at city hall is magnificent, too, with domed steeples and a clock.

One day, there's a knock on the door. I see a man, standing there. I know him. It's my other missing uncle, Isaac, called Itch, who also had been taken by the Russian army.

"*Voo? Voo?*" I'm saying. *Wójek* is Polish for "uncle." It's pronounced "voo-yek." But I'm so shocked, I can't get the whole word out.

"Yes, Lola, it's me," he says.

Uncle Itch, along with another cousin who survived, is part of my family now, too.

We don't stay in Kraków that long, only about a year. This is not so surprising. After living in so many towns, each new one seems more like a stopover, not a destination. But now Poland itself is no longer our destination. Uncle George wants to leave. Everybody in that house wants to leave. Tension between the Poles and the Jews has not gone away.

Rosa leaves the country before I do — first she goes to Hungary, then to Czechoslovakia, and France, and as far away as Venezuela, before arriving in America.

America is our new destination.

The next few months, when we ourselves leave Poland, we live in a series of different towns and cities. Some places are so bombed out, they are little more than dust and rubble. Along the way, Jewish relief committees provide us with schools and sleeping quarters. All temporary, of course. So many Jewish people are in transit, on the move, unsettled. Everything has a fleeting, spur-of-the-moment feeling to it.

Without the right papers, we have to cross into Czechoslovakia illegally, at night. We go on foot, with cartons of cigarettes to bribe guards every step of the way. Cigarettes are as good as money. We stay in Prague for a while. Then we get on a train and go to Vienna, Austria, a place that has special meaning for anyone from Czortków.

Czortków, in its 400-year-old history, has had many different governments, as borders changed and new treaties were signed. At one time, it was actually under Turkish rule. For almost 150 years, it was Austrian. I can remember hearing some of the older people in town speak German, because Czortków only became Polish in 1918, 16 years before my birth. Now, after the war, Czortków has become Ukrainian, as it remains today. Its

Ukraine name is Chortkiv. *Ukraine* is a word that means "borderline" or "on the edge." That seems fitting.

As a little girl, I thought there was a permanent connection between Poland and Czortków, but in fact it lasted only 26 years. It's strange, to be Polish when my hometown is no longer part of Poland. It's just as strange to know that Czortków, the town I was born in and loved, no longer wanted me.

I have never been back to Czortków, or to any other part of Ukraine. I have no desire to go.

At the end of 1946 and the beginning of 1947, we stay in the town of Eschwege, Germany, in a displaced persons' (DP) camp, one of many run by the United Nations. This one is not far from Frankfurt, which has a lot of Americans. For me, the DP camp is great. It's set up with barracks, and we all live in one big room. I have lots of friends, lots of freedom — perfect for a 12-year-old! There's a Hebrew school where I learn Hebrew songs. I go to the movies in town. I can feel the sun on my face. I get a new cousin — my aunt gives birth to a boy, Norman.

I don't have the words for it, or even the concept, but this is where I start to "come out of myself." It's a beginning, anyway.

The dress is still, and always, with me. I'm much too big for it now, but I never part with it.

At the DP camp, there's a Zionist organization called Betar. I sign up to go to Israel, because I have decided I want to go there, not America. Uncle George gets mad at me and takes my name off the list.

"You have no business going to Israel alone!" he tells me. "You're twelve, for heaven's sake!"

To me, it seems only natural to make a huge decision like that, by myself. Twelve — or 22 — what's the difference? I've been on my own since the day I pretended to be a mute.

Uncle George gets in touch with relatives in the United States — cousins of Babcia's. These cousins are two older men, brothers named Jack and Isaac (also, like my uncle, called Itch) Rosenblatt. You have to have a sponsor to come to America, and the brothers agree to sponsor us. But only a certain number of people get approved every year. My uncle and aunt and their children are approved right away. I am not.

But my aunt and uncle won't go without me.

The DP camps themselves are only temporary. Uncle Itch and my cousin travel to Cyprus and eventually to Israel. Whoever hasn't left the DP camp has to go live in Kassel, a German city. We stay there a few months. Uncle George wants me to learn English; he hires someone with an British accent to tutor me once a week. So I learn a little English to go along with my Polish, my Russian, and the bits I know of Yiddish, Hebrew, and Ukrainian.

Finally, I receive permission to go to America. We leave on July 7, 1949, from Bremen, Germany, on a converted military troop transport ship called *General S. D. Sturgis.* I'm violently seasick, throwing up the whole journey. Eleven days later, we arrive in Boston. With my new knowledge of English, I go to a market to buy some tomatoes. But my pronunciation is more British than American, I say "to-MAH-toes." What I must sound like, with my Polish-British accent!

That evening we take a train to New York City, to Grand Central Terminal, where Jack and Itch will meet us. I have to go down an escalator. I've never seen anything like it. Stairs that move — coming out of nowhere and disappearing at the top? I get so scared!

Jack lives in a house on Kings Highway in Brooklyn. Itch lives in the Bronx. We stay with Jack until Uncle George finds an apartment for us in Manhattan, on the Lower East Side. This is my first home in America — a two-bedroom walkup, four flights up.

I get to know the neighborhood — the many shops on Delancey Street, which spill out onto the sidewalk. There's a library near my house. At first, I borrow only Polish books. *That's not going to get me anyplace in America,* I realize. So I switch to English books.

During the summer, I stay with Jack's and Itch's grown children, each week with a different family. One of their sons, who lives in the suburbs, is an accountant. His home is jaw-droppingly gorgeous. *This is how people can live in America,* I think. *Nice! But I'll never be able to live the way they do.*

They don't speak Polish, and I'm not allowed to speak Yiddish with any of them, only English. Some of the grandchildren are teenagers. They have friends over. I see boys and girls flirting, having fun. *What am I going to do here in America?* I think. *I'll never fit in, never. Will I ever have a boyfriend? I'll never have a boyfriend!*

In October, I'll be 15. I'm a teenager; I'm becoming a young woman. But in many ways I feel like a tiny child all over again. I can walk, but that's about the only thing I know for sure. The language, the culture, all the little daily things I'm used to, the foods with the unfamiliar tastes I've never tasted before ... What are Rice Krispies? What's a chicken pot pie? And Chinese food! I have to learn everything new.

In September, I start school — Seward Park High School on Essex Street in Manhattan. There are so many newly arrived European kids that special classes are set up for non-English speakers. We take a test. By now, my English isn't too bad, and I can even say "tomatoes" the way Americans do. So, right away, I'm put in a regular English class.

Life isn't so easy. Uncle George is now making leather pocketbooks, not boots. He earns only $45 a week. I never have an allowance; there's never any money in my pocket; I don't want to ask my aunt or uncle for it. If I want a drink or something to eat on the street, I can't buy anything. Other relatives purchase my clothes. It's harder to be poor in a rich country than it was to be poor in a poor country. Also, my aunt and uncle aren't getting along. They fight all the time. Sometimes I call Cousin Jack in Brooklyn to see if I can stay with him for a few days — just to get away from the yelling.

My next-door neighbors have a small business selling nylon stockings. After school and on weekends, I work in their store. My job is to change the word *irregular,* which means the stockings have a flaw — maybe one leg is shorter than the other, or something — to *regular,* which means they are perfect. Do I know that what I'm doing is not right? I do! But the job allows me finally to have a little money, and also I can contribute to the household.

I come down with bad headaches and a sore throat. I go by myself to a dispensary on Essex Street, where I can get free medical care. The doctors tell me I have badly infected tonsils, and they've got to come out. I schedule an appointment. I take care of it myself, as I have learned to do.

But I ask my aunt to pick me up after the operation.

Basically I make my own decisions. There are little rules I have to follow — my uncle won't let me wear lipstick, that kind of thing — but when it comes to the big stuff, I do that myself. Over the summer, I take classes in Manhattan, to learn how to use a comptometer — a big, old metal counting machine with button keys, used by bookkeepers and accountants, an early version of a calculator. I don't go back to high school — I want to be independent! I want to have enough money, so I don't have to think about it all the time. It takes me a year to get my certificate, and now, in 1950 when I'm 16, I am a genuine comptometer operator.

I end up going back to high school at night and working during the day. Saks 34th Street, a big department store, has a whole section of comptometer operators. I sit at my desk, along with dozens of other women, clicking away at the machines, adding up the day's sales.

But it's hard to work by day and go to school at night, so I drop out of school again. And why not? Nobody's telling me to drop out or not to drop out.

When I'm 17, I go to Brighton Beach, near Coney Island, with a bunch of my friends. There's a man there, with a bunch of his friends. His name is Walter Kaufman. He's 11 years older than I am and works in the garment center. Turns out he's also from Poland. We start to go steady — *I have a boyfriend!* — and we get engaged on my eighteenth birthday. Walter wants to wait a year to get married, but we marry in six months, because I really want to get out of the house. My aunt and uncle divorce soon after I'm married. Uncle George ends up going to the altar a total of five times! That includes the wife in Lwów who was murdered by the Germans.

Now that I'm older, and married, and maybe a little smarter, I think that not having a high school diploma is terrible. I return to school and get my high school diploma.

Walter and I move into a little one-bedroom apartment in Brooklyn. I work until 1955, when I'm 21 and pregnant with my first child, Deborah Renee. Many Jewish people name their children after people who have died. Deborah is named for my mother, Dwojra (the Hebrew name for Deborah), and her middle name is for Walter's mother, Rachel. In 1958, our son Michael Jay is born, named for Walter's father (Michael) and for my father (Jidle). Walter has gone to school and is now designing and creating patterns for coats and suits. We start looking around for a bigger place. We move out to the suburbs, to a house on Long Island. *Look at me,* I think. *I'm living like an American!* In 1966, our third child, Jeffrey Scott, is born. He is named for my father's father, Jakov, and for my oldest uncle, Shmil.

Uncle George is like a grandfather to my children. He gets along with them so beautifully. Actually, Uncle George gets along with everybody — except his wives.

My husband hid during the war, too.

Walter was born in 1923, and grew up in the little Polish town of Połaniec — the "ł" is pronounced like a "w." Połaniec is so small that when the Germans arrived, the town itself was the ghetto. The Germans only sent one or two soldiers there. But the Germans weren't really the problem. As a 19-year-old in 1942, Walter, along with his two brothers, was hiding from his fellow Poles.

For one winter he, too, hid in a hole in a barn. But only by day. At night, he and his brothers could climb out of the hole and stretch their legs.

When we are first married, I don't speak with Walter about my wartime experiences, which are still so painful to me. He doesn't press me.

CHAPTER NINE ✡

After the war, many hidden children — those in Europe, those in America, those in Israel — have something in common: silence. The years pass; hidden children grow up. They don't discuss what happened to them with their friends. They fall in love and get married. They don't talk about the war years with their husbands and wives. They have children of their own. They don't tell their children.

How many children were hidden? Somewhere between 10,000 and 500,000. Why is the number so inexact? As one history book points out, nobody knows how many hidden children and their helpers were discovered and killed — records weren't kept of such things. And how could you make a list of those who were so young when they went into hiding that they just grew up with their hiding families and were never even told they were Jews? Or count the number of those who survived but never came forward to identify themselves as hidden children? All you can say is: There are probably some among us now who have stayed silent to this day.

After the war, hidden children are told, "You were lucky. You survived."

Because so many did not survive.

Six million Jews of the nine million who were living in Europe in 1939 died in the Second World War. A million and a half were children. Adults had about a 33 percent chance of surviving. Children had only a 10 percent chance.

In Poland, three million Poles died, along with more than three million Jews. Of the original 3.3 million Jews in Poland, only 300,000 were still alive on V-E day. Of the one million Jewish children in pre-war Poland, there were only 5,000 left. Polish Jews had the worst losses in Europe. In Czortków, 99 percent of the Jews were gone.

"You were lucky. You survived."

But it's hard to feel lucky. We did what we could and what seemed to make sense, but even when things went right, we were scared every moment. That's not what "lucky" feels like.

Many hidden children had to keep moving from one hiding place to the next. I only had to move once myself — from a farmhouse room to a hole under a barn — but one child actually moved 30 times. Many hidden children had to take on new, non-Jewish identities: This made one woman feel so torn apart from her true self that she now says, "I was a fictitious child." Another hidden child now says that we were "old people with children's faces, without a trace of joy, happiness, or childish innocence." Some never got over the fact that there were no safe places for their parents to run to, and that while they themselves were hiding, their parents died. Years later, one woman still thinks her father is crouched outside her house, scared to knock on her door. Another orphan, a boy, spends years wondering if the "special speaker" coming to his school assemblies will turn out, this time, to be his father. Even among the children who are later reunited with their parents, many remain strangers to one another. A girl finds herself calling her father "Mister."

For nearly 50 years I don't and can't speak about what has happened to me — not to Walter, not to anyone. I was silent when I was hidden, and I stay silent even when I'm not. Happiness comes, but it does not lead to talking. Until —

What changes for me?

On Memorial Day weekend in 1991, I attend the first International Gathering of Children Hidden During World War II at the Marriott Marquis Hotel in Times Square, in New York City. There are 1,600 people there, listening to panels and lectures, and attending workshops, where they can share their experiences of hiding — experiences that were so solitary and distancing.

I meet Jane Marks, a reporter for *New York* magazine. She wants to interview me for a book she's writing on hidden children. We sit down with each other; we talk on the phone. She asks me questions. I let the story out. I allow the words to come. The feelings, too. Jane Marks opens the floodgates, in more ways than one. I cry every time I speak with her! Her book is published in 1993. I am no longer silent, at least in print.

In 2001, I get a letter from the United States Holocaust Memorial Museum in Washington, D.C. They are looking for artifacts, items that somehow survived the war, to display in a large exhibit. I decide to donate my dress. Amazingly, the dress has suffered no damage to speak of. The white cloth has turned a bit yellow, and there are some spots, but that's all. It is as beautiful as ever.

My daughter, Deborah, doesn't want me to part with the dress. "I want it for myself," she says.

"But, Deb," I say, "it's just hanging in my closet. If I give it to you, it'll just be hanging in your closet. Maybe it's time that someone else sees it."

"I guess you're right, Mom," she says.

By now, Walter and I are living in New City, north of New York City, in suburban Rockland County, New York. I fill out papers for the Holocaust Museum. A woman curator arranges to meet me in Manhattan, only an hour or so away. I show her the dress, wondering what she'll think of it. I can't believe how thrilled she is! The dress goes on display for a year. And not just in Washington, D.C. We travel to many cities together, that dress and I.

In one city, at a reception for the exhibit, someone asks me, "What made you decide to give up the dress?"

I don't want to answer.

I'm with Sara Bloomfield, the director of the Holocaust Museum. She hands me a microphone, and says, "Go ahead and talk."

It sort of falls into my lap at that moment, the whole notion that I will speak in public. Well, I simply have to, with all those people staring at me and that microphone in my hand.

In the next city, Sara just hands me the microphone and says, again, "Go ahead and talk."

My silence, it seems, has been fully broken.

Ever since, I have spoken on many occasions at schools and synagogues. I was such a shy, quiet child — the personality that cloaked me, the personality that I knew, even then, I wasn't supposed to have. Later, in my happy, busy years as a comptometer operator or a mother, I still had that cloak on, deep inside.

Not anymore. I've given away the dress and taken off the cloak.

Looking back now, surrounded by the love of my family — our children are grown and have college degrees, successful careers, and children of their own — I am astonished, endlessly, by Anna Aksenczuk's bravery.

As with everything else, exact numbers can never be known, but it has been estimated that one percent of the non-Jewish population in Europe helped Jews. Most of the rescuers were Christian, but in places like Yugoslavia, a country with a large Islamic population, Muslim families also extended help to Jews. In every country with Jews, some Jews were hidden — by the French, the Dutch, the Bulgarians, the Poles, Ukrainians, Belgians, Italians, Greeks, Danes, Hungarians, and Germans. The German government executed 100 Ukrainians for the crime of hiding Jews, and many more all over Europe. But for every rescuer who was exposed and killed, there were many others, like Anna Aksenczuk, whose efforts were successful. What they did was as hard as it was brave — because they had to seem to be living entirely normal lives even while doing something no one does in normal times.

Some of the non-Jews who risked their lives, and the lives of their families, in order to save Jews during the Second World War, are honored in Israel as "The Righteous Among the Nations." On November 21, 1994, Anna Aksenczuk was officially recognized as one of the "righteous." So, too, was her son, Bohdan, who fed us, and her husband, Evstahi. I never even knew, until all these many decades later, that Anna had a husband. I certainly didn't know that I owe my life to him, too.

I ask myself now, if the situation were reversed and I were in Anna's place, would I do what she did? Maybe it's an impossible question to answer in the abstract or in advance. Because it's really a question of asking yourself, *Would the world ever make sense again if I don't do this thing?* Before the war, if Anna had been asked, would you risk everything for the lives of a few Jews? she might have answered either way — and in either case it would have been just words. Yet, when faced with the real-life situation in a real-life war, she found she had to say yes. Maybe she didn't even know she had this enormous capacity inside her, this "righteousness," until it came time for her to use it.

CHAPTER TEN ✡

On June 26, 1962, after living in America for 13 years, I open my newspaper, *The New York Post,* and get a shock. There's an article with the headline: NAZI OFFICER GETS LIFE IN 9 MURDERS.

I read:

Saarbrücken, Germany. A district court today sentenced former S.S. Sgt. Kurt Köllner, 58, to life in prison after finding him guilty of murdering nine Jews in Poland during World War II.... Köllner was charged with killing Jews while assigned to Nazi security police at Czortków ... in 1942 and 1943. His defense attorney, who argued for acquittal on grounds of doubt, is expected to appeal.

Life in prison! I have never seen the name of Czortków in the New York papers, and suddenly the news has reached me here, that my mother's murderer will be going to jail. For so many who died, their stories remain unfinished, and their murderers are never identified or held accountable. Yet, in my case, society has made it plain that a crime was committed and must be paid for. A German court — a German court! — has looked 20 years into the past to reject the cruelty, the pain, the wrongness of the day my mother was shot. It's almost as if the Germans have lit a candle to her memory.

Nowadays, I spend as much time as I can with my grandchildren — Roxanne and Eliana (Debbie's daughters), and Hannah (Michael's daughter), and Gabriel (Jeffrey's son). I read a lot. Like my mother, I'm good with my hands. I can embroider, knit, and crochet. I do yoga. I didn't like it in the beginning — I couldn't wait for that first class to be over — but I stayed with it. Now I breathe so deeply, I can feel the air fill my lungs. I play mah-jongg, a Chinese tile game of skill and strategy that may have been invented by Confucius. I like a fast-moving game. When I play with people who are going too slowly, I tell them, "Come on, guys, you're playing like beginners. Play like a pro!"

I don't think I have much of an accent. Sometimes people, when they meet me, can't place me. Once I was asked, "Are you from Boston?" Must have been that day I spent there!

Rosa Sirato, my friend in Kraków, is still a friend. She lives only a half hour's drive away.

Dolo, who was in the hole with me, lives in Israel now. All these many years later, we are in touch. I've even spoken on the phone with Bohdan, who still lives in Czortków.

And I still see people I befriended in the displaced persons' camp in Eschwege.

I love my life, but there are still things inside me that are fragile. If something doesn't happen when it's supposed to happen, for instance.

My daughter calls me every morning at ten o'clock. One morning she calls at eleven. I'm in a panic. "Is everything all right?" I ask her.

"Yeah, calm down," she says.

"But you're calling at eleven, not ten!" I say.

"So what? Everything's fine!"

She has quite a time, settling me down.

Sometimes I open the refrigerator door, just to look at the food.

I have a new life, but the old life is always with me.

My home is full of light and surrounded by leafy trees. Walter has a garden in the yard. He grows zucchini, tomatoes, cucumbers, and peppers. He's created bird feeders that attract doves, blue jays, cardinals. For the sparrows and robins, he's built the most amazing birdhouses. There are, at last count, 10 of them. They look like miniature multilevel homes, painted in bold reds and blues, on top of tall poles. I call them bird condos. To keep out the squirrels, Walter has constructed lampshadelike collars that sit about halfway up the poles.

In the spring, all the birdhouses have baby birds in them and anxious parents. As the days lengthen, I love seeing the next generation of birds, first half-size and hesitant, and then fully grown, coming and going as they please, flying out of the birdhouses and into the bright expanse of the sky.

DEDICATIONS AND ACKNOWLEDGMENTS

To the memory of my mother, my father, my grandparents, and my family who perished in the Holocaust. I dedicate this book especially to my grandmother Ekka, who saved my life, and to my uncle George, who raised me, and to my cousin Ethel, who was the sister I never had.

I still can't believe I've finally opened up and can talk about my life during the war! Thanks to my family and friends who kept encouraging me. I'd like to thank Carole Goodman, from the temple in Mahwah, New Jersey; she asked me to speak one Friday evening. In the audience, at the right place at the right time, was Roy Wandelmaier, an editor at Scholastic. Many thanks to Roy for taking the story of my life and turning it into a book. Thanks to Lois Metzger for her patience and cooperation and for being so nice.

— L.R.K.

To the memory of Gordon Hunter, a Scottish
beekeeper who welcomed and took care
of my mother, a 16-year-old Jewish girl
from Vienna, during the war.

Special thanks to Roy Wandelmaier, my editor at
Scholastic, who brought me into this project.
Thanks, too, to Lola Rein Kaufman, for sharing her
story, and for her bravery, resilience, and humor, and
for being such a lovely person.
— L.M.

BOOKS AND WEB SITES OF INTEREST

Here are some books and Web sites that shine light on the previously shadowed world of hidden children, on the part of Europe that Lola Rein Kaufman comes from, and also on Lola herself. — L.M.

Bluglass, Kerry. *Hidden from the Holocaust: Stories of Resilient Children Who Survived and Thrived.*
Westport, Connecticut: Praeger Publishers, 2003.
A scholarly look at how children endure unbearable hardships, yet grow into adults who are happy and well-adjusted. Kerry Bluglass brings the more than a dozen people she interviews to vivid life.

Cretzmeyer, Stacy. *Hidden Child of the Holocaust: A True Story.*
New York: Scholastic Inc., 1999.
The moving story of a five-year-old girl in France who must leave everything behind and take on a whole new identity in hiding.

Czerniewicz-Umer, Teresa, Malgorzata Omilanowska, and Jerzy S. Majewski. *Eyewitness Travel: Poland.*
New York: DK Publishing, Inc., 2001.

A look at modern-day Poland and a look back to tenth-century Poland, with dazzling photographs.

Czortków ShtetLinks Web Site. http://www.shtetlinks. jewishgen.org/Suchostaw/sl_czortkow.htm
Click on this Web site to read about Lola's birthplace — Czortków, Poland. There are photographs here, past and present, and Abraham Morgenstern's beautiful memoir, a book-length appreciation of a place that lost its humanity — "Chortkov Remembered: The Annihilation of a Jewish Community." Also included is Rose Kalishar's testimonial to Anna Aksenczuk, and one woman's harrowing description of deportation from Czortków in the town's first "action."

Evans, Andrew. *Ukraine: The Bradt Travel Guide.* Guilford, Connecticut: The Globe Pequot Press Inc., Second Edition, 2007.
Czortków, Poland, is now part of Ukraine. This guidebook details the fascinating history and culture of the area. Gorgeous photographs.

Frank, Anne. *The Diary of a Young Girl: The Definitive Edition.* Edited by Otto H. Frank and Mirjam Pressler. Translated by Susan Massotty.

New York: Anchor Books, 1996.
Anne Frank hid with her parents and sister, and another
family, on the top floors of her father's office building in
Amsterdam. During her more than two years in hiding,
Anne kept a diary. It's this amazing diary, read by more than
25 million people in 70 languages, that has made Anne Frank
the world's most famous "hidden child." Anne died in a
concentration camp at age 15.

Greenfeld, Howard. *The Hidden Children.*
Boston: Houghton Mifflin Company, 1993.
Spectacular, haunting look at the hidden children of Europe,
including many first-person narratives and photographs.

Johnstone, Sarah. *Ukraine.*
Victoria, Australia: Lonely Planet Publications Pty Ltd, 2005.
Informative, insightful guidebook to Ukraine.

Marks, Jane. *The Hidden Children: The Secret Survivors of the
Holocaust.*
New York: Fawcett Columbine, 1993.
Jane Marks was the first person to elicit Lola's story, and
devotes a chapter to Lola in her book. Lola's friend in

Kraków, Rosa Sirota, is also interviewed here. There are 23 voices in all. A far-reaching, tremendously important book.

Meltzer, Milton. *Rescue: The Story of How Gentiles Saved Jews in the Holocaust.*
New York: HarperCollins Publishers, 1988.
One of the earliest books about hidden children, and one of the best. In simple, elegant, unsentimental language, Milton Meltzer writes about non-Jewish people who risked their lives to help Jews during the war.

Metzger, Lois. *Yours, Anne: The Life of Anne Frank.*
New York: Scholastic Inc., 2004.
A biography of Anne Frank that looks at her whole life, from her birth to her death, including the diary years and the effects her diary has had on the world ever since.

Opdyke, Irene Gut, with Jennifer Armstrong. *In My Hands: Memories of a Holocaust Rescuer.*
New York: Alfred A. Knopf, 1999.
Remarkable true-life story of a young Polish woman who saved the lives of more than a dozen Jews in the war.

Rosenberg, Maxine B. *Hiding to Survive: Stories of Jewish Children Rescued from the Holocaust.*
New York: Clarion Books, 1994.
Fourteen people tell their stories here, and the stories are unforgettable. A wonderful book.

Stallings, Douglas, ed. *Fodor's Poland.*
New York: Fodor's Travel Publications, 2007.
Excellent guidebook that transports the reader to Poland, region by region.

United States Holocaust Memorial Museum. "Silent Witness: The Story of Lola Rein and Her Dress." http://www.ushmm. org/museum/exhibit/online/silentwitness/lola/flash/index. htm
An elegant, essential Web site. Here is Lola's dress, which the museum has lovingly preserved and restored. The stitched flowers that Lola's mother so skillfully embroidered are on full display. On video, Lola speaks about her experiences — being in the dark hole, killing lice, and the humiliation of begging for food after liberation.